50 Healthy Breakfast Meal Recipes

By: Kelly Johnson

Table of Contents

- Overnight Oats with Chia Seeds and Berries
- Greek Yogurt Parfait with Granola and Honey
- Avocado Toast with Poached Egg
- Quinoa Breakfast Bowl with Almonds and Fruit
- Smoothie Bowl with Spinach and Banana
- Whole Wheat Banana Pancakes
- Chia Pudding with Coconut Milk and Mango
- Egg Muffins with Spinach and Feta
- Sweet Potato Hash with Eggs
- Overnight Buckwheat Porridge with Nuts
- Cottage Cheese with Pineapple and Walnuts
- Veggie Omelette with Bell Peppers and Onions
- Almond Butter and Banana Smoothie
- Oatmeal with Apple and Cinnamon
- Breakfast Burrito with Black Beans and Avocado
- Smashed Chickpea Toast with Dill
- Healthy Breakfast Cookies with Oats and Raisins
- Quinoa and Berry Breakfast Bake
- Savory Oatmeal with Spinach and Parmesan
- Fruit Salad with Mint and Lime
- Zucchini Bread Overnight Oats
- Whole Grain Waffles with Fresh Berries
- Buckwheat Pancakes with Maple Syrup
- Green Smoothie with Kale and Avocado
- Poached Eggs over Quinoa and Spinach
- Yogurt Bowl with Flaxseed and Sliced Almonds
- Peanut Butter Overnight Oats with Banana
- Baked Eggs in Avocado
- Smoothie with Greek Yogurt and Mixed Berries
- Almond Flour Muffins with Blueberries
- Savory Quinoa with Roasted Vegetables
- Breakfast Chia Seed Pudding with Almond Milk
- Whole Grain Toast with Hummus and Cherry Tomatoes
- Nutty Granola with Dried Fruits
- Berry and Spinach Smoothie
- Egg and Avocado Breakfast Bowl

- Cauliflower Rice Breakfast Stir-Fry
- Coconut Yogurt with Granola and Seeds
- Rice Cakes with Almond Butter and Sliced Apples
- Pumpkin Spice Oatmeal
- Breakfast Tacos with Scrambled Eggs and Salsa
- Toasted Muesli with Yogurt and Fresh Fruit
- Chocolate Protein Pancakes
- Roasted Vegetable Frittata
- Banana and Nut Butter Smoothie
- Oatmeal with Nut Butter and Sliced Bananas
- Millet Porridge with Almond Milk and Berries
- Sautéed Greens with Eggs
- Quinoa Fruit Salad
- Muesli with Dried Fruits and Nuts

Overnight Oats with Chia Seeds and Berries

Ingredients:

- 1/2 cup rolled oats
- 1 tablespoon chia seeds
- 1 cup milk (or dairy-free alternative)
- 1/2 cup mixed berries (fresh or frozen)
- Honey or maple syrup (to taste)

Instructions:

1. **Combine Ingredients:** In a jar or bowl, mix rolled oats, chia seeds, and milk. Stir well.
2. **Add Sweetener:** Add honey or maple syrup if desired, and mix again.
3. **Refrigerate:** Cover and refrigerate overnight.
4. **Serve:** In the morning, top with mixed berries before enjoying.

Greek Yogurt Parfait with Granola and Honey

Ingredients:

- 1 cup Greek yogurt
- 1/2 cup granola
- 1/2 cup mixed berries (or fruit of choice)
- Honey (to drizzle)

Instructions:

1. **Layer Ingredients:** In a glass or bowl, layer Greek yogurt, granola, and mixed berries.
2. **Repeat Layers:** Repeat the layers until all ingredients are used.
3. **Drizzle Honey:** Finish with a drizzle of honey on top.
4. **Serve:** Enjoy immediately!

Avocado Toast with Poached Egg

Ingredients:

- 1 ripe avocado
- 2 slices whole-grain bread
- 2 eggs
- Salt and pepper
- Red pepper flakes (optional)
- Lemon juice (optional)

Instructions:

1. **Toast Bread:** Toast the slices of whole-grain bread until golden brown.
2. **Mash Avocado:** In a bowl, mash avocado with a fork. Add salt, pepper, and a splash of lemon juice if desired.
3. **Poach Eggs:** In a pot of simmering water, gently crack in the eggs and poach for about 3-4 minutes until whites are set.
4. **Assemble:** Spread mashed avocado on toasted bread and top with poached eggs. Sprinkle with red pepper flakes if desired.

Quinoa Breakfast Bowl with Almonds and Fruit

Ingredients:

- 1 cup cooked quinoa
- 1/2 cup almond milk (or milk of choice)
- 1/2 banana, sliced
- 1/4 cup almonds, chopped
- 1 tablespoon honey or maple syrup (optional)

Instructions:

1. **Combine Quinoa and Milk:** In a bowl, combine cooked quinoa and almond milk. Heat if desired.
2. **Add Toppings:** Top with banana slices, chopped almonds, and honey or maple syrup if using.
3. **Serve:** Enjoy warm or cold.

Smoothie Bowl with Spinach and Banana

Ingredients:

- 1 banana
- 1 cup spinach (fresh or frozen)
- 1/2 cup Greek yogurt (or dairy-free alternative)
- 1/2 cup almond milk (or milk of choice)
- Toppings: granola, sliced fruit, nuts, seeds

Instructions:

1. **Blend Ingredients:** In a blender, combine banana, spinach, Greek yogurt, and almond milk. Blend until smooth.
2. **Serve in Bowl:** Pour into a bowl and add your favorite toppings.
3. **Enjoy:** Enjoy with a spoon!

Whole Wheat Banana Pancakes

Ingredients:

- 1 cup whole wheat flour
- 1 tablespoon baking powder
- 1 tablespoon sugar (optional)
- 1/4 teaspoon salt
- 1 cup milk (or dairy-free alternative)
- 1 banana, mashed
- 1 egg
- 1 tablespoon melted butter (or oil)

Instructions:

1. **Mix Dry Ingredients:** In a bowl, whisk together whole wheat flour, baking powder, sugar, and salt.
2. **Combine Wet Ingredients:** In another bowl, mix milk, mashed banana, egg, and melted butter.
3. **Combine Mixtures:** Pour wet ingredients into dry ingredients and stir until just combined.
4. **Cook Pancakes:** Heat a skillet over medium heat and pour in batter. Cook until bubbles form, then flip and cook until golden.
5. **Serve:** Serve warm with maple syrup or fresh fruit.

Chia Pudding with Coconut Milk and Mango

Ingredients:

- 1/4 cup chia seeds
- 1 cup coconut milk
- 1 tablespoon maple syrup (or honey)
- 1 ripe mango, diced

Instructions:

1. **Mix Chia Pudding:** In a bowl, combine chia seeds, coconut milk, and maple syrup. Stir well.
2. **Refrigerate:** Cover and refrigerate for at least 4 hours or overnight until thickened.
3. **Serve:** Top with diced mango before enjoying.

Egg Muffins with Spinach and Feta

Ingredients:

- 6 eggs
- 1 cup fresh spinach, chopped
- 1/2 cup feta cheese, crumbled
- Salt and pepper
- Optional: diced bell peppers, onions, or tomatoes

Instructions:

1. **Preheat Oven:** Preheat oven to 350°F (175°C). Grease a muffin tin.
2. **Whisk Eggs:** In a bowl, whisk together eggs, salt, and pepper. Stir in spinach and feta (and any optional ingredients).
3. **Pour Mixture:** Pour egg mixture into muffin tin, filling each cup about 3/4 full.
4. **Bake:** Bake for 20-25 minutes or until eggs are set.
5. **Serve:** Let cool slightly before removing from the tin. Enjoy warm or chilled.

Sweet Potato Hash with Eggs

Ingredients:

- 2 medium sweet potatoes, diced
- 1 red bell pepper, diced
- 1/2 onion, chopped
- 2 tablespoons olive oil
- Salt and pepper
- 4 eggs
- Fresh parsley (for garnish)

Instructions:

1. **Cook Sweet Potatoes:** In a large skillet, heat olive oil over medium heat. Add sweet potatoes and cook until tender, about 10-15 minutes.
2. **Add Vegetables:** Stir in bell pepper and onion. Season with salt and pepper, and cook until veggies are softened.
3. **Cook Eggs:** Create small wells in the hash and crack an egg into each well. Cover the skillet and cook until eggs are set to your liking.
4. **Serve:** Garnish with fresh parsley and serve warm.

Overnight Buckwheat Porridge with Nuts

Ingredients:

- 1 cup buckwheat groats
- 2 cups almond milk (or milk of choice)
- 1 tablespoon maple syrup (optional)
- 1/4 cup mixed nuts, chopped
- Fresh fruit (for topping)

Instructions:

1. **Combine Ingredients:** In a jar or bowl, combine buckwheat groats, almond milk, and maple syrup. Stir well.
2. **Refrigerate:** Cover and refrigerate overnight.
3. **Serve:** In the morning, top with chopped nuts and fresh fruit before enjoying.

Cottage Cheese with Pineapple and Walnuts

Ingredients:

- 1 cup cottage cheese
- 1/2 cup pineapple chunks (fresh or canned)
- 1/4 cup walnuts, chopped
- Honey (optional, for drizzling)

Instructions:

1. **Combine Ingredients:** In a bowl, combine cottage cheese, pineapple chunks, and walnuts.
2. **Serve:** Drizzle with honey if desired and enjoy.

Veggie Omelette with Bell Peppers and Onions

Ingredients:

- 3 eggs
- 1/2 bell pepper, diced
- 1/2 onion, diced
- Salt and pepper
- 1 tablespoon olive oil
- Fresh herbs (optional, for garnish)

Instructions:

1. **Sauté Vegetables:** In a skillet, heat olive oil over medium heat. Add bell pepper and onion, cooking until softened.
2. **Whisk Eggs:** In a bowl, whisk together eggs, salt, and pepper.
3. **Cook Omelette:** Pour eggs over the vegetables in the skillet. Cook until set, folding the omelette in half as it cooks.
4. **Serve:** Garnish with fresh herbs if desired and serve warm.

Almond Butter and Banana Smoothie

Ingredients:

- 1 banana
- 2 tablespoons almond butter
- 1 cup almond milk (or milk of choice)
- 1 tablespoon honey (optional)
- Ice cubes (optional)

Instructions:

1. **Blend Ingredients:** In a blender, combine banana, almond butter, almond milk, and honey. Add ice if desired.
2. **Serve:** Blend until smooth and serve immediately.

Oatmeal with Apple and Cinnamon

Ingredients:

- 1 cup rolled oats
- 2 cups water or milk
- 1 apple, diced
- 1 teaspoon cinnamon
- Sweetener (honey or maple syrup, to taste)
- Optional toppings: nuts, raisins, or seeds

Instructions:

1. **Cook Oats:** In a pot, bring water or milk to a boil. Stir in oats, diced apple, and cinnamon. Reduce heat and simmer for about 5 minutes, stirring occasionally.
2. **Sweeten:** Add sweetener to taste.
3. **Serve:** Serve warm, topped with your choice of nuts or seeds.

Breakfast Burrito with Black Beans and Avocado

Ingredients:

- 1 large tortilla
- 1/2 cup black beans, rinsed and drained
- 1/2 avocado, sliced
- 1/4 cup shredded cheese (optional)
- 2 eggs, scrambled
- Salsa (for serving)

Instructions:

1. **Cook Eggs:** In a skillet, scramble the eggs until cooked through.
2. **Assemble Burrito:** On a tortilla, layer black beans, scrambled eggs, avocado slices, and cheese if using.
3. **Wrap Burrito:** Roll the tortilla tightly, folding in the sides as you go.
4. **Serve:** Slice in half and serve with salsa.

Smashed Chickpea Toast with Dill

Ingredients:

- 1 cup canned chickpeas, rinsed and drained
- 1 tablespoon olive oil
- 1 tablespoon lemon juice
- Fresh dill, chopped
- Salt and pepper
- Whole-grain bread (for toasting)

Instructions:

1. **Mash Chickpeas:** In a bowl, mash chickpeas with a fork. Stir in olive oil, lemon juice, dill, salt, and pepper.
2. **Toast Bread:** Toast slices of whole-grain bread until golden brown.
3. **Assemble Toast:** Spread the chickpea mixture on the toasted bread.
4. **Serve:** Enjoy immediately, garnished with extra dill if desired.

Healthy Breakfast Cookies with Oats and Raisins

Ingredients:

- 1 cup rolled oats
- 1/2 cup almond flour (or whole wheat flour)
- 1/2 cup mashed banana (about 1 medium banana)
- 1/4 cup honey or maple syrup
- 1/2 cup raisins
- 1/2 teaspoon cinnamon
- 1/4 teaspoon salt
- 1/2 teaspoon vanilla extract

Instructions:

1. **Preheat Oven:** Preheat your oven to 350°F (175°C) and line a baking sheet with parchment paper.
2. **Mix Ingredients:** In a bowl, combine oats, almond flour, mashed banana, honey, raisins, cinnamon, salt, and vanilla. Mix well.
3. **Form Cookies:** Drop spoonfuls of the mixture onto the baking sheet, flattening them slightly.
4. **Bake:** Bake for 12-15 minutes until golden. Let cool before serving.

Quinoa and Berry Breakfast Bake

Ingredients:

- 1 cup cooked quinoa
- 2 cups mixed berries (fresh or frozen)
- 2 eggs
- 1/2 cup milk (or dairy-free alternative)
- 1 tablespoon maple syrup
- 1 teaspoon vanilla extract
- 1 teaspoon cinnamon

Instructions:

1. **Preheat Oven:** Preheat your oven to 350°F (175°C) and grease a baking dish.
2. **Combine Ingredients:** In a bowl, mix cooked quinoa, berries, eggs, milk, maple syrup, vanilla, and cinnamon.
3. **Bake:** Pour the mixture into the baking dish and bake for 25-30 minutes until set.
4. **Serve:** Let cool slightly before serving.

Savory Oatmeal with Spinach and Parmesan

Ingredients:

- 1 cup rolled oats
- 2 cups vegetable broth or water
- 1 cup fresh spinach
- 1/4 cup grated Parmesan cheese
- Salt and pepper to taste
- Optional: fried egg for topping

Instructions:

1. **Cook Oats:** In a pot, bring vegetable broth or water to a boil. Stir in oats and cook for about 5 minutes.
2. **Add Spinach:** Stir in spinach and cook until wilted. Season with salt and pepper.
3. **Serve:** Serve topped with Parmesan cheese and a fried egg if desired.

Fruit Salad with Mint and Lime

Ingredients:

- 2 cups mixed fresh fruit (such as berries, melons, and citrus)
- Juice of 1 lime
- 1 tablespoon honey (optional)
- Fresh mint leaves, chopped

Instructions:

1. **Combine Ingredients:** In a bowl, mix fresh fruit, lime juice, honey, and mint.
2. **Serve:** Toss gently and serve chilled.

Zucchini Bread Overnight Oats

Ingredients:

- 1/2 cup rolled oats
- 1/2 cup grated zucchini
- 1/2 cup milk (or dairy-free alternative)
- 1 tablespoon chia seeds
- 1 tablespoon maple syrup
- 1/2 teaspoon cinnamon
- Optional toppings: nuts, raisins, or shredded coconut

Instructions:

1. **Combine Ingredients:** In a jar or bowl, mix rolled oats, grated zucchini, milk, chia seeds, maple syrup, and cinnamon.
2. **Refrigerate:** Cover and refrigerate overnight.
3. **Serve:** In the morning, top with your choice of toppings.

Whole Grain Waffles with Fresh Berries

Ingredients:

- 1 cup whole wheat flour
- 1 tablespoon baking powder
- 1 tablespoon sugar (optional)
- 1 cup milk (or dairy-free alternative)
- 1/4 cup melted coconut oil (or butter)
- 1 egg
- Fresh berries for serving

Instructions:

1. **Preheat Waffle Maker:** Preheat your waffle maker according to manufacturer's instructions.
2. **Mix Dry Ingredients:** In a bowl, combine whole wheat flour, baking powder, and sugar.
3. **Mix Wet Ingredients:** In another bowl, whisk together milk, melted coconut oil, and egg.
4. **Combine Mixtures:** Pour wet ingredients into dry and stir until just combined.
5. **Cook Waffles:** Pour batter into the preheated waffle maker and cook until golden brown. Serve with fresh berries.

Buckwheat Pancakes with Maple Syrup

Ingredients:

- 1 cup buckwheat flour
- 1 tablespoon baking powder
- 1 tablespoon sugar (optional)
- 1 cup milk (or dairy-free alternative)
- 1 egg
- 2 tablespoons melted butter or oil

Instructions:

1. **Mix Dry Ingredients:** In a bowl, combine buckwheat flour, baking powder, and sugar.
2. **Mix Wet Ingredients:** In another bowl, whisk together milk, egg, and melted butter.
3. **Combine Mixtures:** Pour wet ingredients into dry and stir until just combined.
4. **Cook Pancakes:** Heat a skillet over medium heat and pour in batter. Cook until bubbles form, then flip and cook until golden brown.
5. **Serve:** Serve with maple syrup.

Green Smoothie with Kale and Avocado

Ingredients:

- 1 cup kale leaves, stems removed
- 1/2 avocado
- 1 banana
- 1 cup almond milk (or milk of choice)
- 1 tablespoon honey (optional)
- Ice cubes (optional)

Instructions:

1. **Blend Ingredients:** In a blender, combine kale, avocado, banana, almond milk, and honey. Add ice if desired.
2. **Serve:** Blend until smooth and serve immediately.

Poached Eggs over Quinoa and Spinach

Ingredients:

- 1 cup cooked quinoa
- 2 cups fresh spinach
- 2 eggs
- 1 tablespoon olive oil
- Salt and pepper
- Optional: hot sauce or red pepper flakes

Instructions:

1. **Sauté Spinach:** In a skillet, heat olive oil over medium heat. Add spinach and cook until wilted. Season with salt and pepper.
2. **Poach Eggs:** In a separate pot, bring water to a gentle simmer. Crack each egg into a small bowl and gently slide into the water. Poach for about 3-4 minutes until the whites are set.
3. **Assemble:** In a bowl, layer cooked quinoa and sautéed spinach. Top with poached eggs.
4. **Serve:** Drizzle with hot sauce or sprinkle with red pepper flakes if desired.

Yogurt Bowl with Flaxseed and Sliced Almonds

Ingredients:

- 1 cup Greek yogurt
- 2 tablespoons flaxseed
- 1/4 cup sliced almonds
- Fresh fruit (such as berries or banana)
- Honey (optional)

Instructions:

1. **Combine Ingredients:** In a bowl, add Greek yogurt, flaxseed, and sliced almonds.
2. **Top with Fruit:** Add your choice of fresh fruit on top.
3. **Sweeten if Desired:** Drizzle with honey if desired and enjoy!

Peanut Butter Overnight Oats with Banana

Ingredients:

- 1/2 cup rolled oats
- 1 cup milk (or dairy-free alternative)
- 1 tablespoon peanut butter
- 1/2 banana, sliced
- 1 tablespoon chia seeds (optional)
- Honey or maple syrup (optional)

Instructions:

1. **Mix Ingredients:** In a jar or bowl, combine rolled oats, milk, peanut butter, banana slices, and chia seeds.
2. **Refrigerate:** Cover and refrigerate overnight.
3. **Serve:** In the morning, stir and add additional honey or maple syrup if desired.

Baked Eggs in Avocado

Ingredients:

- 1 ripe avocado, halved and pitted
- 2 eggs
- Salt and pepper
- Optional toppings: salsa, cheese, or herbs

Instructions:

1. **Preheat Oven:** Preheat your oven to 425°F (220°C).
2. **Prepare Avocado:** Scoop out a little extra avocado from each half to make room for the egg. Place avocado halves in a baking dish.
3. **Add Eggs:** Crack an egg into each avocado half. Season with salt and pepper.
4. **Bake:** Bake for 15-20 minutes until eggs are cooked to your liking.
5. **Serve:** Top with salsa, cheese, or herbs if desired.

Smoothie with Greek Yogurt and Mixed Berries

Ingredients:

- 1 cup mixed berries (fresh or frozen)
- 1/2 cup Greek yogurt
- 1 cup almond milk (or milk of choice)
- 1 tablespoon honey (optional)
- Ice cubes (optional)

Instructions:

1. **Blend Ingredients:** In a blender, combine mixed berries, Greek yogurt, almond milk, and honey. Add ice if desired.
2. **Serve:** Blend until smooth and serve immediately.

Almond Flour Muffins with Blueberries

Ingredients:

- 2 cups almond flour
- 1/4 cup honey or maple syrup
- 3 eggs
- 1/4 cup almond milk (or milk of choice)
- 1 teaspoon baking powder
- 1 cup blueberries (fresh or frozen)

Instructions:

1. **Preheat Oven:** Preheat your oven to 350°F (175°C) and line a muffin tin with paper liners.
2. **Mix Wet Ingredients:** In a bowl, whisk together almond flour, honey, eggs, almond milk, and baking powder.
3. **Fold in Blueberries:** Gently fold in blueberries.
4. **Bake:** Divide the batter into the muffin tin and bake for 20-25 minutes until golden and a toothpick comes out clean.
5. **Cool:** Let cool before serving.

Savory Quinoa with Roasted Vegetables

Ingredients:

- 1 cup cooked quinoa
- 2 cups mixed vegetables (such as bell peppers, zucchini, and carrots)
- 2 tablespoons olive oil
- Salt and pepper
- Optional: feta cheese or nuts for topping

Instructions:

1. **Preheat Oven:** Preheat your oven to 425°F (220°C).
2. **Roast Vegetables:** Toss mixed vegetables with olive oil, salt, and pepper. Spread on a baking sheet and roast for 20-25 minutes until tender.
3. **Combine:** In a bowl, combine cooked quinoa and roasted vegetables.
4. **Serve:** Top with feta cheese or nuts if desired.

Breakfast Chia Seed Pudding with Almond Milk

Ingredients:

- 1/4 cup chia seeds
- 1 cup almond milk (or milk of choice)
- 1 tablespoon maple syrup (optional)
- Fresh fruit or nuts for topping

Instructions:

1. **Combine Ingredients:** In a jar or bowl, mix chia seeds, almond milk, and maple syrup.
2. **Refrigerate:** Cover and refrigerate for at least 4 hours or overnight until thickened.
3. **Serve:** Top with fresh fruit or nuts before enjoying.

Whole Grain Toast with Hummus and Cherry Tomatoes

Ingredients:

- 2 slices whole grain bread
- 1/2 cup hummus
- 1 cup cherry tomatoes, halved
- Olive oil, for drizzling
- Salt and pepper
- Fresh herbs (optional, for garnish)

Instructions:

1. **Toast Bread:** Toast the whole grain bread until golden.
2. **Spread Hummus:** Spread hummus generously on each slice.
3. **Top with Tomatoes:** Arrange cherry tomato halves on top of the hummus.
4. **Season and Serve:** Drizzle with olive oil, season with salt and pepper, and garnish with fresh herbs if desired.

Nutty Granola with Dried Fruits

Ingredients:

- 2 cups rolled oats
- 1/2 cup nuts (almonds, walnuts, or pecans), chopped
- 1/2 cup seeds (pumpkin or sunflower)
- 1/4 cup honey or maple syrup
- 1/4 cup coconut oil, melted
- 1/2 teaspoon cinnamon
- 1 cup dried fruits (raisins, cranberries, or apricots)

Instructions:

1. **Preheat Oven:** Preheat your oven to 350°F (175°C).
2. **Mix Dry Ingredients:** In a large bowl, combine oats, nuts, seeds, and cinnamon.
3. **Add Wet Ingredients:** In another bowl, mix honey (or maple syrup) and melted coconut oil. Pour over the dry ingredients and stir until well combined.
4. **Bake:** Spread the mixture on a baking sheet and bake for 20-25 minutes, stirring halfway through, until golden.
5. **Cool and Add Fruit:** Allow to cool, then stir in dried fruits. Store in an airtight container.

Berry and Spinach Smoothie

Ingredients:

- 1 cup fresh spinach
- 1 cup mixed berries (fresh or frozen)
- 1 banana
- 1 cup almond milk (or milk of choice)
- 1 tablespoon honey (optional)

Instructions:

1. **Blend Ingredients:** In a blender, combine spinach, mixed berries, banana, almond milk, and honey.
2. **Serve:** Blend until smooth and serve immediately.

Egg and Avocado Breakfast Bowl

Ingredients:

- 2 eggs
- 1 ripe avocado, diced
- 1 cup cooked quinoa or brown rice
- Salt and pepper
- Red pepper flakes (optional)
- Fresh herbs (optional, for garnish)

Instructions:

1. **Cook Eggs:** Poach, scramble, or fry the eggs to your preference.
2. **Assemble Bowl:** In a bowl, layer quinoa or brown rice, diced avocado, and cooked eggs.
3. **Season and Serve:** Season with salt, pepper, and red pepper flakes. Garnish with fresh herbs if desired.

Cauliflower Rice Breakfast Stir-Fry

Ingredients:

- 2 cups cauliflower rice (fresh or frozen)
- 1 cup mixed vegetables (bell peppers, peas, carrots)
- 2 eggs
- 2 tablespoons soy sauce or tamari
- Olive oil, for cooking
- Green onions, for garnish

Instructions:

1. **Sauté Vegetables:** In a skillet, heat olive oil over medium heat. Add mixed vegetables and cook until tender.
2. **Add Cauliflower Rice:** Stir in cauliflower rice and cook for another 3-4 minutes.
3. **Scramble Eggs:** Push the mixture to one side of the skillet, crack the eggs into the empty side, and scramble until cooked.
4. **Combine:** Mix everything together, add soy sauce, and stir to combine. Serve warm, garnished with green onions.

Coconut Yogurt with Granola and Seeds

Ingredients:

- 1 cup coconut yogurt

- 1/2 cup granola
- 2 tablespoons mixed seeds (chia, pumpkin, or sunflower)
- Fresh fruit (for topping)

Instructions:

1. **Layer Ingredients:** In a bowl, layer coconut yogurt, granola, and mixed seeds.
2. **Top with Fruit:** Add your choice of fresh fruit on top.
3. **Serve:** Enjoy immediately!

Rice Cakes with Almond Butter and Sliced Apples

Ingredients:

- 2 rice cakes
- 2 tablespoons almond butter
- 1 apple, sliced
- Cinnamon (optional, for sprinkling)

Instructions:

1. **Spread Almond Butter:** Spread almond butter evenly on each rice cake.
2. **Top with Apple Slices:** Arrange sliced apples on top of the almond butter.
3. **Serve:** Sprinkle with cinnamon if desired and enjoy.

Pumpkin Spice Oatmeal

Ingredients:

- 1 cup rolled oats
- 2 cups water or milk (or dairy-free alternative)
- 1/2 cup pumpkin puree
- 1 teaspoon pumpkin pie spice
- 1 tablespoon maple syrup (optional)
- Chopped nuts (for topping)

Instructions:

1. **Cook Oats:** In a pot, bring water or milk to a boil. Stir in rolled oats, pumpkin puree, and pumpkin pie spice. Reduce heat and simmer for about 5 minutes, stirring occasionally.
2. **Sweeten:** Stir in maple syrup if desired.
3. **Serve:** Serve warm, topped with chopped nuts.

Breakfast Tacos with Scrambled Eggs and Salsa

Ingredients:

- 4 small corn or flour tortillas
- 4 eggs
- 1/4 cup milk
- Salt and pepper, to taste
- 1/2 cup salsa (store-bought or homemade)
- Optional toppings: avocado, cheese, cilantro

Instructions:

1. **Scramble Eggs:** In a bowl, whisk together eggs, milk, salt, and pepper. Heat a skillet over medium heat, add a little oil, and pour in the egg mixture. Scramble until just set.
2. **Warm Tortillas:** In a separate skillet, warm the tortillas until soft.
3. **Assemble Tacos:** Divide scrambled eggs among tortillas. Top with salsa and any additional toppings you like.
4. **Serve:** Enjoy warm!

Toasted Muesli with Yogurt and Fresh Fruit

Ingredients:

- 1 cup rolled oats
- 1/2 cup mixed nuts and seeds
- 1/4 cup honey or maple syrup
- 1/2 teaspoon cinnamon
- 1 cup yogurt (Greek or dairy-free)
- Fresh fruit (such as berries, banana, or apple)

Instructions:

1. **Toast Muesli:** Preheat the oven to 350°F (175°C). Spread oats and nuts on a baking sheet, drizzle with honey, and sprinkle with cinnamon. Bake for 10-15 minutes, stirring halfway, until golden.
2. **Cool:** Allow to cool before storing in an airtight container.
3. **Serve:** In a bowl, layer toasted muesli, yogurt, and fresh fruit.

Chocolate Protein Pancakes

Ingredients:

- 1 cup rolled oats (or oat flour)
- 1/2 cup protein powder (chocolate flavor)
- 1 tablespoon cocoa powder
- 1 teaspoon baking powder
- 1 cup milk (or dairy-free alternative)
- 1 egg

- Optional toppings: maple syrup, berries, or banana slices

Instructions:

1. **Mix Ingredients:** In a bowl, combine oats, protein powder, cocoa powder, and baking powder. In another bowl, whisk together milk and egg.
2. **Combine:** Pour the wet ingredients into the dry ingredients and mix until just combined.
3. **Cook Pancakes:** Heat a non-stick skillet over medium heat. Pour batter to form pancakes and cook until bubbles form on the surface, then flip and cook until golden.
4. **Serve:** Serve with your favorite toppings.

Roasted Vegetable Frittata

Ingredients:

- 6 eggs
- 1 cup mixed vegetables (bell peppers, spinach, zucchini, etc.), roasted
- 1/2 cup milk (or dairy-free alternative)
- Salt and pepper, to taste
- Optional: cheese for topping

Instructions:

1. **Preheat Oven:** Preheat your oven to 375°F (190°C).
2. **Whisk Eggs:** In a bowl, whisk together eggs, milk, salt, and pepper.
3. **Combine:** In a greased oven-safe skillet, add roasted vegetables and pour the egg mixture over them. Stir gently to combine.
4. **Bake:** Cook on the stovetop for a few minutes until the edges set, then transfer to the oven and bake for 15-20 minutes until fully set.
5. **Serve:** Let cool slightly, slice, and serve warm.

Banana and Nut Butter Smoothie

Ingredients:

- 1 ripe banana
- 1 tablespoon nut butter (peanut, almond, or cashew)
- 1 cup milk (or dairy-free alternative)
- 1 tablespoon honey (optional)
- Ice cubes (optional)

Instructions:

1. **Blend Ingredients:** In a blender, combine banana, nut butter, milk, honey, and ice if desired.
2. **Serve:** Blend until smooth and pour into a glass. Enjoy!

Oatmeal with Nut Butter and Sliced Bananas

Ingredients:

- 1 cup rolled oats
- 2 cups water or milk (or dairy-free alternative)
- 1 tablespoon nut butter (peanut, almond, or cashew)
- 1 banana, sliced
- Honey or maple syrup (optional)
- Cinnamon (optional)

Instructions:

1. **Cook Oats:** In a pot, bring water or milk to a boil. Stir in rolled oats and reduce heat. Cook for about 5 minutes, stirring occasionally, until creamy.
2. **Add Toppings:** Remove from heat and stir in nut butter. Top with sliced bananas, and drizzle with honey or maple syrup and a sprinkle of cinnamon if desired.
3. **Serve:** Enjoy warm!

Millet Porridge with Almond Milk and Berries

Ingredients:

- 1 cup millet
- 3 cups almond milk (or milk of choice)
- 1/2 teaspoon vanilla extract
- 1 cup mixed berries (fresh or frozen)
- Honey or maple syrup (optional)

Instructions:

1. **Cook Millet:** In a pot, combine millet and almond milk. Bring to a boil, then reduce heat and simmer for about 20 minutes until the millet is tender and the mixture is creamy.
2. **Add Flavor:** Stir in vanilla extract and sweeten with honey or maple syrup if desired.
3. **Serve:** Top with mixed berries and enjoy warm.

Sautéed Greens with Eggs

Ingredients:

- 2 cups mixed greens (spinach, kale, or Swiss chard)
- 2 eggs
- 1 tablespoon olive oil
- Salt and pepper, to taste
- Optional: hot sauce or feta cheese

Instructions:

1. **Sauté Greens:** In a skillet, heat olive oil over medium heat. Add mixed greens and cook until wilted. Season with salt and pepper.
2. **Cook Eggs:** In a separate pan, cook the eggs to your preference (fried, poached, or scrambled).
3. **Assemble:** Plate the sautéed greens and top with the cooked eggs. Add hot sauce or feta cheese if desired.

Quinoa Fruit Salad

Ingredients:

- 1 cup cooked quinoa (cooled)
- 1 cup mixed fresh fruit (berries, melon, kiwi, etc.)
- 1 tablespoon honey or maple syrup
- Juice of 1 lime
- Fresh mint leaves (optional, for garnish)

Instructions:

1. **Combine Ingredients:** In a large bowl, mix together cooked quinoa, mixed fruit, honey or maple syrup, and lime juice.
2. **Serve:** Toss gently and serve chilled or at room temperature. Garnish with fresh mint if desired.

Muesli with Dried Fruits and Nuts

Ingredients:

- 1 cup rolled oats
- 1/2 cup mixed nuts (almonds, walnuts, or hazelnuts), chopped
- 1/2 cup dried fruits (raisins, cranberries, or apricots)
- 1 cup milk (or dairy-free alternative)
- Honey or maple syrup (optional)

Instructions:

1. **Mix Ingredients:** In a bowl, combine rolled oats, mixed nuts, and dried fruits.
2. **Add Liquid:** Pour milk over the muesli and let it soak for a few minutes to soften the oats.
3. **Sweeten:** Drizzle with honey or maple syrup if desired and enjoy!

www.ingramcontent.com/pod-product-compliance
Lightning Source LLC
LaVergne TN
LVHW081510060526
838201LV00056BA/3030